THOUGHTS FOR A WOEBEGONE NIGHT

Thoughts for a Woebegone Night

Jessin Jayan

First published by Jessin Jayan 2024

Copyright © 2024 by Jessin Jayan

All rights reserved. No part of this publication may be reproduced, stored, or transmitted in any form or by any means, electronic, mechanical, photocopying, recording, scanning, or otherwise without written permission from the publisher. It is illegal to copy this book, post it to a website, or distribute it by any other means without permission.

First edition

ISBN: 979-8-218-49167-3

Editing by Maisy Wilkinson
Cover art by Kiran Roy

To Amma, for reading me my first stories
To Pappa, for working hard to give us a good life

Contents

1. Preface — 13
2. Poetry — 15
3. Heart Eater — 16
4. Life — 17
5. Solitude — 18
6. Reflection — 20
7. Temptations — 21
8. Chaos — 22
9. Strangers — 23
10. Underneath a Mask — 25
11. Rebirth — 26
12. December — 27
13. Scars — 28
14. Blinded — 29
15. Wish — 30
16. Confession — 31
17. Stargazing — 32
18. LDR — 33
19. Insomnia — 34
20. Makeup — 35
21. Pluviophile — 36
22. Melancholy — 37
23. Memories — 38
24. Coffin — 39
25. On the Fence — 40
26. B/W — 42

27. Revelation	43
28. Muse	45
29. A Bottle of Sorrow	46
30. Thorns	48
31. Her	49
32. Realization	50
33. A Parley With My (Ruthless) Mind	52
34. Penpal	53
35. Temptress	54
36. Chasing Sunsets	55
37. Sinner	56
38. Cliche	57
39. 1920	59
40. Cigerattes and Coffee	60
41. Skin	61
42. The Last Gospel	62
43. Travelers	63
About Author	65

Preface

For you dear reader, these might be some poems arranged well on paper. But for me, they're confessions. They're unspoken words and untold emotions that I kept to myself and hid under a facade.
The poems you're about to read are about memories. Some faded and some that I will never forget. It's about the places I've been, the people I've met, and the things I've done.

As you read through these poems, you will see pain and love. You may sense the fractures and failures that have led to the creation of these poems. Amidst these emotions, I also want you to see hope. A light that might not be obvious or prominent but exists all the same. Whenever I did get a glimpse of it, I held on to it. And it carried me through all these years. I can only wish that the same light will carry you to a better tomorrow.

Poetry

my silence gave birth to words
those words weren't filled with voice but ink
curated with my deepest emotions
darkened like my rage and pain
liquefied, like the tears down my cheek
and I spilled it on a stained old paper

Heart Eater

was it her dreamy smile or her marble eyes
that drew me to her?
I can't recall
it had been so long since the heart eater left
after her meal

in the trance of love that she put me in,
I was her lover, her butler, and the meal
it was with my lips I showed her love
in my arms she found closure

listening to my heartbeat, she embraced me
on hot, sweaty lustful nights we lost ourselves
she taught me how to dream
and then I showed her those dreams through my poems

in her chest, I found the warmest of nights
in her absence, my world and I were frozen still
her beautiful long fingers exploring my body,
like in ecstasy I melt
placing her warm hand on my beating heart
her marble eyes staring into my soul

then she ripped my heart out of my chest
it had her name on it
still beating as she pushes her teeth in
chewing, slurping, licking all with her dreamy smile,
still placed on her face

as I lay dead with a lost look on my pale face
she smiled at me and kissed me goodbye with her bloody lips
I was her lover, her butler
I was a meal for the heart eater

Life

life is like a poem
it is a verse that has many interpretations
it is cryptid
sometimes good, sometimes bad
and I am merely a word among the verse

still have a lot to write before I go
even after I'm gone, the poem will flow like the life it is
new interpretations, new riddles, new words
there will even be new verses
and a synonym would have taken my place
but the poem will still flow like the life it is

Solitude

yes, I'm surrounded by people
I can hear them as they speak to me
but then why do I feel alone?
I'm not the only one in this room, yet why do I feel lonely?
is it because I had to say goodbye to you last night?
I didn't want to, yes. but we did it anyway

under this cherry tree, I sit
counting the ones that kiss the earth
would they be saying sweet goodbyes to the ones still holding?
would they be missing the ones that had to be let go?
maybe they're keeping me company, coming down to say hi to me
perhaps they realize that I'm lonely
something you could never see

yes, I had to walk away from my friends and family
maybe I was selfish, or maybe I was trying to find meaning
maybe I was looking for means to mend my broken heart
saying goodbye to them was the hardest part

I still listen to the songs we sang together
think about the time you left me alone
sometimes I come here to sit under the cherry tree
my hands are cold now, last time you were here to hold me

as the leaves whisper to my ears in the wind
as these fallen ones embrace me with greetings
I look back in time and think about the moments I've spent alone
the songs we sang together, the goodbyes I had to say which was harder,
the people who left me behind, I think about all of them

as the cold breeze kisses my skin,
a teardrop falls on my hand
and I just sit here alone,
watching everyone I love, walking away from me.

Reflection

I looked in the mirror,
I saw greed- not pride
I saw hate- not love
I saw despair- not hope
I saw someone else- not myself
and then I turned around
slowly walked away and realized,
somewhere between madness and death
I lost myself.

Temptations

my demons are like spiders and they know how to weave
I am just prey and naive enough to fall
one after another I sin impetuously
carrying this shame and guilt on my shoulders

the weight of it holds me down
stuck in their web unable to free myself
me a sinner, feeding my demons, I sin again,
they close in for more and more
it's like I'm in a labyrinth, and the walls are temptations
I run, I stumble, I fall, I sin and when they get closer, I repeat

making them stronger and I grow weak
can't turn around now, I'm in too deep
it comes in waves, whispers, and thoughts unfeasible
it is relentless my adversary and I'm weak in my soul
an obstacle in my path to redemption
I run, I stumble, I fall and I sin

there is no hope in the darkness
my habitual sins feed my demons
and they weave stronger, closing in faster
so I run, I fall, I sin and I repeat

Chaos

there is a war in my head
in my chaotic heart
lurking demons inside me,
I'm all messed up.

Strangers

I remember a time when we used to be everything but strangers
some songs reminded me of you and made me smile
but now I cry
my pen wrote love letters for you
now it's out of ink like I'm out of love
the poems I read were about the sweet love you showed me
and now it's heartbreak
the movies I watched were about us
and now it's a drama with tears

you left saying it's not me but isn't it true
that it was my fault?
you left me all our memories
along with my late-night tears
I used to smile at the happy ones
but now they're all just sad
trust me, erasing all your memories from my phone didn't help
guess my mind doesn't have a delete button for me to press

I'm sorry for all the times I've hurt you,
now you're gone and it's too late for an apology
you said this isn't permanent before you left
you said you might come back after a while
and that was three years ago on a sad evening
I couldn't sleep that night but I hope you did
after all, you have to make up for all the nights
we stayed awake laughing

do you still have the letters I wrote you?
where we talked about traveling the world together
I still have the ones you've sent me
but I never touched them since you left
I couldn't read them even if I did,

my tears would blind me
and ruin your beautiful cursive words

that's all I have now of yours,
besides your memories you trusted me with
I dust them from time to time in my dreams,
I cherish them while I listen to songs
and I wipe my tears until the next time

tell me, will I ever talk to you again?
so I could apologize a million times for the mess I made
tell me will there be an 'Us' again?
or is it just 'You' and 'Me'?

Underneath a Mask

'how are you so blissful and amusing?
so 'over the moon' and charming?
even at the hardest of times,
you seem calm and soothing!'

and she said,

'maybe I am too good at pretending.'

Rebirth

hope is the ember you see at the end of sadness
it is a flicker waiting to go ablaze
and it's your longing for better tomorrows that fuels it

hope is a silent prayer
it is the gleam of light in your dusk
it's the hand that carries you
when your sorrow's burden exceeds
hope is the promise of a new day
and your optimism is its lover

it is what motivates you
faith; is its truthful warrior
wipe your tears because they kill the ember
hold your faith against your heart
let your optimism fuel the flame
now burn bright until you're dead and reborn

December

hold my hand
we can hide under this blanket
come closer to me
we can sit near the fireplace
let me look at you
let me taste those lips
let's make love like dewdrops of December

Scars

she was trembling and shaking
weeping and shivering
the grasp of her demon,
she tumbled down screaming
it was eating her from the inside
feeding on her dark side
she tried to get it out,
she tried to get rid of it,
but all that was left, were some bleeding cuts

Blinded

your eyes were dreamy
your lips, strawberries
your words were candies
your voice, a melody

your touch was fondly tender
your skin, soft as a feather
your body is like a flowing river
your hair, dark as a moonless night

your smile was a ray of sunlight
even when you cried you looked beautiful as that
how much I've known you and how much I've seen
oh dear, I saw everything except the truth you hid from me

I was dreaming of a time when we'll be together
thought of the places we could have visited
but yes we were far from each other
and now it's like that forever

I couldn't see what was about to happen
I might have been busy building dreams
and now you're gone, and all that's left are the dreams I built
which is already all shattered and there's nothing but debris

Wish

I wish I could forget just like you did
I wish I could move on just like you said
but every time I try hard for that,
your memories return like it was yesterday

Confession

I'm sorry
I loved you
I'm sorry- I cared about you
I'm sorry
for being nice to you
I'm sorry
that I couldn't hurt you
forgive me dear, for I have sinned

Stargazing

her fingers pointed to the sky
showing me all the constellations
under the pine trees, together on a rock,
we are two bodies but intertwined souls

her voice was like a soothing whisper in my ear
her smile more beautiful than the night
she was into stars and I couldn't take my eyes away
not from the sky but from her flowing hair

my heartbeat was louder than the dark woods
our fingers kissing each other
my shoulder was her pillow
her delicate embrace-my blanket

we both stole warmth from each other
gazing at the stars and the fireflies
they looked like stars came down from the sky
her excitement was immeasurable and I was falling once again

the cold breeze ran its fingers on my skin waking me up
still sitting on that rock but no more fireflies
with a sigh, I look up and the stars are gone
reached for your hand and realized so were you

LDR

you just turned into my best part
you became my beloved best half
but I'm sorry dear, that we are miles apart.

Insomnia

I used to sleep, to forget the pain
to escape reality,
to be free from my fears,
one could only think that it would help

to let sleep takeover
to just forget and to let go
I embrace the darkness and slowly fall asleep
and here it comes,
my worst nightmares

Makeup

cigarette stain hiding under her lipstick
bruise marks under her makeup
bitings and nail scratches on her back
stitches on her shattered heart
she was beautiful.

Pluviophile

coursing over my skin,
dripping through my hair,
dewdrops of rain
hugging me like I'm unaware

just like an old tale
the rain came by my way
with the sweet smell of fresh monsoon soil
healing me and wiping my tears,
once again another rainy day

Melancholy

like nimbus clouds, she cloaks my soul in the dark
tried to articulate but it was in vain
it was the silence that constricted me
and in my loneliness, she struck me down

moment after moment I become pale
slowly yet surely she choked my hopes away
I tried to catch my breath but couldn't
slithering on my skin feeding on my tears

it's time; there's no escape for me
the smiling mask breaks apart
it's the victory of my enemy
no more spectacle the curtain falls

a deathly warm embrace won me
still slithering but she has claimed my numb soul
in the moment of sweet victory, she called me
'Mine'
with a cold tear on my cheek, I called her
'Misery'

Memories

your memories always hit me hard
and I fall every time
grab me and pull me closer
wrap your arms around me
hold me tight
so I can rest my head on your chest

now stab me with your smile
let me bleed without denial
then allow me to die again and again
until we're reborn together once again

Coffin

then I closed my eyes in pain
getting colder inside my veins
slowly falling asleep again
not to wake up but to fade away

On the Fence

I wish I could be better than this,
I wish I could be someone else,
so here I am on the edge of sanity,
about to fall into the hands of insanity

a change is inevitable yet comes too late
it's time to seize what's in my grasp
it's long overdue to make the jump
maybe I am contemplating, maybe even procrastinating
but maybe, just maybe I'm afraid of the unknown

here I am suffocating yet safe and sound
who knows what lies on the other side if I jump?
what if I perish? what if I fall into a never-ending oblivion?
the dilemma is killing me yet not literally
I'm safe on the fence, I'm safe until I jump

but what if I flourish? It's hard, my mind is like a pendulum,
swinging from questions to doubts
from what's known to unknown
but what if I make the jump?
what if I survive and the unknown reveals itself to me?

it might be insane, scary even but it's long overdue to let go of the fence
it's time for me to fly and make a life on the other side
my legs shivering, and I can feel the chills running up my spine
I have to let go of the fence and jump
is there an utopia waiting or is it me being dumb?

only one way to find out if I could just let go
if only I could make that jump and land on my feet
my heart rising, my mind rushing to regain control of my thoughts

it's time to jump.
maybe I will perish, maybe I will keep on falling,
into the depths of the unknown

but maybe, just maybe I will find my utopia
I will find love and maybe I will live
only one way to find out

B/W

the red in my love started to fade
my purple dreams turned into gray
all of my colors, covered under a shade
why is everything black and white?

Revelation

I've drowned in the lake of misery
fated to suffer in the valley of pain
I've prayed; screamed his name
confessed my sins and begged to be saved

'Eli, Eli, lama sabachthani? — My God my
God, why have you forsaken me?'
I walked into your house and saw your face
my arms raised to you along with my eyes
do you see me? Or am I not worthy?

remember the day I first came to see you?
remember how my mother taught me to praise you?
I remember how I lit those candles
how I stood next to your alter
I became a part of you and you became a part of me

now I'm far away from you and lost
searching for an answer that you won't grant
even then, here I am on my knees with nothing to give but my faith
and then came my revelation;

when the world crucified me
you were on my side, already on that cross
when my tears were unstoppable
you were crying with me
when I was wounded and broken
you were hurting beside me
when I couldn't sleep and when I was restless
you stayed with me and listened

I wiped my tears and stood on my feet
eyes still on your beautiful bloody face

I know now that I'm not lost
you were always with me even at my lowest

I hear you now
I hear you in a breeze, I hear you in the waves
in the morals my mother gave me
in all the love that still surrounds me
I hear you now in all the prayers chanting
and I hear you in all the silence sneaking

Muse

we held our hands under shooting stars
we kissed after 'I do' in front of the altar candles
we snuggled down on winter nights
we gazed at each other and fell again
love of my life- my muse

A Bottle of Sorrow

it hurts so bad
all my pain inside
deep down my throat,
choking in a concentrated form
feeling thirsty;
drowning in my mind
a burning sensation, a black hole
let me dilute it with some alcohol

one is not enough I pour myself another one
now the pain is more intense
I can still see your face
I can still remember the things you said
I can't take this anymore the glass fills up with another pour

my heart aches and now I'm sobbing
my tongue feels numb but my mind does not
why do I still hear your voice in my head?
why do I still see your smile like you're here?

one more; not on the rocks give it to me strong
my hands are weak and my mouth feels dry
yet I chugged it like a man dying from thirst
your face is blurred now
your voice distorted
my mind is wandering like a floating cloud on a windy day
I see shapes like pareidolia, trying to make a meaning but can't
are you gone yet?

please don't visit me tonight in my dream
I'm tired of waking up to realize it was just that, nothing more
my eyes grow weary, my body shuts down
are you gone yet?

good; take your memories with you
memories; where we were more than just strangers
where I felt something for you that I never felt before
where you smiled at me with compassion
no, you're not gone. your memories are still with me

quick, finish that bottle
I need every last drop
I gather the strength to grab that glass
drinking it as fast as I can
empty bottle rolling on the floor
now let me sit back

my words broken, my mind scrambled
I don't recognize my surroundings
my eyes welcomed the darkness
did I finish every last drop?
my hands are too weak yet I made sure

are you gone yet? good;
now let me sleep, let me forget,
let me escape and let me fall

Thorns

she reminded me of roses
her body is like the curves of its petals
her smile made the roses jealous
she smelled like a bouquet of them
and I wanted to hold her

in the trance of love and lust
I embraced her against my heart
like a beautiful rose, she bloomed
but I forgot about the thorns
so I bled

Her

I found art once. the kind you can rarely find on earth
her hair is like autumn
her eyes hazel like they hold mysteries
her smile is the dawn of my dusk
she's like never-ending poetry
and I'm merely just a reader

her words are warm flames to my cold heart
and it's in her sweet lips I find my peace
it's in her happiness my purpose lies
she's the painting that I can never finish yet is perfect

her touch revives me
it's in her arms I find shelter
she is the heaven I seek
all the answers to my uncertainties
the light in my darkness
and the constellation guiding my nights

Realization

what hurt you the most?
what leaves you dead inside?
what makes you feel empty and lost?
isn't it when you realize,
no matter how hard you try,
no matter how much you mean it,
sometimes you'll never be good enough?

isn't it true, that you can give your absolute best
yet end up losing what you value the most?
isn't it true and cruel that you care and love
yet you end up invisible?

you show empathy and you give compassion
yet isn't it true that you are left alone with nobody to return the favor?
sometimes life can be cruel that way,
or at least someone once said so

yet isn't it true that you keep going?
isn't it true that you let others take advantage?
you value everyone else more than yourself
yet isn't it true they see you as worthless?
you smile at their cruel jokes, you let it pass even when it hurts
yet tell me isn't it true that you cry when no one's looking?

you ask others how they feel,
you give them a shoulder to stay up and heal
yet isn't it true that you fall and there's no one to hold you?
isn't it true that you get close too fast?
even though you know it's not gonna last

isn't it true that you give them your attention?
yet you get none in return

so tell me, isn't it true that maybe it's time to let go?
isn't it true that you need to focus on yourself and not on your foe?
isn't it true that you're strong enough?
not for them and not for anyone else but you,
isn't it true that you're good enough?

A Parley With My (Ruthless) Mind

'it's time to stop' I command my mind
like a stereopticon, it projects my grounds
'I've had enough give me back my smile'
'here you go' it grands me wakeful nights

'can't I just be happy for once?'
'not yet, you are sad for life'
sniveling fretful 'yes indeed I'm sad'
'oh yes, here we go with the tears, what a delight?'
'am I in a loop forever?
right after one, you grant me another
it's never-ending, all these reasons to mourn'

'there's a colossal cluster of reasons in here
we have to let them go before we explode
let the fire of rage and anger go down
make them drenched with your tears and
wipe them away
slowly in time, let's cry to sleep and wake'

'you're right, here are my tears'
falling onto my pillow as I lay
cold in my heart, numb in my mind
'think I'm finally falling asleep'

'yes, let the warm hands of sleep take you away
where you don't have to feel the pain of the day
deeper and deeper asleep as you fall
I will meet you at 3 on Dream's behalf
show you all the things you try to forget
all the moments in life you wish would fade
so at 4, we could resume our talk
as you wake up crying and can't fall back'

Penpal

every week I waited for your letters
the weeks I got it, I was the happiest
and when I didn't it was agony
you wrote me about a place I've never been to
the things you've been doing, that made me laugh
and I wrote you back with an excitement
like never before

we shared stories, some happy but not all
I hid hugs among the lines I wrote back
I hope you found them; I certainly found the ones you sent
the more we wrote to each other, the more we knew
but I've never seen you, yet I was in love with your stories

among your lines, I made a face for you,
you looked beautiful
and one week the letter didn't come
I waited another but it was in vain
I wanted to give up but I waited longer
and it felt like an eternity

for the first time, I missed someone I'd never seen before
I felt a lot of emotions but I couldn't name any
and one day your letter came
you told me the reasons but I didn't care
I was so happy that I couldn't wait to write back

today we're not far away from each other
as you lay on my chest reading the letters we wrote,
I realize this
I love you today, and I will love you tomorrow
just how I loved you yesterday before I even saw you

Temptress

under the sheets two souls but one body
the sweet symphony of us becoming one
you draw pictures on my back with your nails
you give yourself to me in this moment of passion
desires coming alive with the ardor of mine for your curves

I am an explorer and you are the fulfillment of lust,
I've been seeking
like on a piano my hands on your skin
longing for the sweet honey from your lips

the cigarettes I've burned
are cold in front of the warmth of your breasts
the bourbons I sipped,
couldn't comprehend the inebriation you gave me
all the pleasure known to mankind together,
can't stand the contentment you put on my body

oh love, you're a flame that burns me
like the wick of a candle
once you find your destination
on this prurient journey of yours
I will be just a cloud of smoke
embracing your naked, enticing body

Chasing Sunsets

never can I catch up
yet I chase the sunset
hoping that one day
I might get close enough to feel the warmth
maybe then it won't be so cold inside me anymore

won't you slow down?
just for once, won't you let me feel alive?
there she goes past the mountains
leaving me and my cold heart behind

Sinner

in the pleasure of my sin
in the ecstasy of my mischief
I close my eyes with a smile on my face,
like I conquered empires

what did I truly gain?
nothing
what did I lose?
everything
everything I am and everything I was supposed to be
lost among my sins

in this hell I conquered
in this chaos, I won
I sit on my throne of shame
the innocence I've crushed
the hearts I've broken
the sweetness I've turned to bitterness
I am sorry, but it is not enough
it never will be

who have I become?
I am nothing but a carrier of guilt
nothing but a sinner who lost himself
waiting for mercy which I don't deserve
even death wouldn't be just for my sinful soul
for I deserve worst, for I am the worst

Cliche

among a million cliches in my life,
I never thought I would feel what I felt that day
the moment I laid my eyes on you
the moment we hugged, I felt something I shouldn't have
did my heart skip a beat? I couldn't tell

I never wished for a day to never end,
like I did on that day
as you were soaking up the sun,
admiring the explosion of colors it left in the sky
I swear I wished you were mine

as your fingers fix up your hair, kissed by the wind
I prayed you would know what I felt
the stories we shared
the nonstop conversations
the laughs and even the silence with you
I enjoyed it

if only I could meet you again for the first time
if only we could be together in that car just once more
I must be a fool to write a love letter that I can never give
to hope that you felt what I felt
even though it can never be

I hold a heart in my hand,
the most beautiful one that I've ever seen
it was trusted to me,
I can never break it and I never will

yet what I felt with you is true
yet I wish in another world you were mine
never will you hear these words from me

for I have given myself to the one
who gave me the heart I hold
but in the deepest part of my soul,
I hope for even a fragment of time
you felt what I felt

I never got to really know you more
but god, I truly wish I did
if only we had more time
if only we were still in that car,
passing corn fields on a country road
now you are gone
along with the pumpkin scented October wind

someone once told me that love is a choice
and I've made mine a long time ago
yet I wish in another branch of time
I am still in that car with you
I wish that night we spent together was still young

as you read this you might wonder
maybe you will never read this
but if you did, this is my love letter to you
the one you will never receive from me
and only in my grave, I will mourn this cliche of my life

1920

have you ever thought of,
what it would be like living inside a novel?
if only I could open a book and get sucked into the streets of Paris
share an old-fashioned with a girl at a jazz club in New York

how wonderful it would be,
if only I could go back in time
walk under the rain in Seattle
light up a cigarette with a Ronson lighter

I would read a book at a cafe in London
I would fulfill my wildest desires in Berlin
if only I could hide among the lines of a novel
I would not get out of a listening booth in an old vinyl store

I would do a million things that I can still do today
but in the past, all of those would feel different
among the stained pages of a novel, it would all be different
the rain, the music, the streets, the woman, and the wine

it would all be so distinct yet spectacular
it's a lost but great world that we never got to see
but still immortal along the lines of a novel
and that's where I want to be, that's where I belong

Cigarettes and Coffee

one more day of my acting is over
I can take my smiling mask off,
now that I'm off the stage for the day and I'm alone

with a cup of coffee on one hand,
a burning cigarette on the other
I sit here seeking peace that I could never find

I hid my sighs among each hit I took
as I exhale I let go of the worries that haunt me
tried to smother them in a cloud of smoke

"why can't you be just happy?" she asked
it was my eighth cigarette that day
she only knew about the 2nd one I smoked after my act

"you're killing yourself" she said
maybe, or maybe this is my penance
this is my self-flagellation
slowly but surely, piece by piece destroying myself into nothing

"let me be in peace for a minute" I replied
with broken voice, bursting into tears she asked,
"am I not giving you peace?" then she slammed the door

"its not you, my love, its me" I thought
with every smoke I fill my lungs,
I'm punishing myself for all the guilt I carry

let me be alone when I do my penance
when I commit self-flagellation
when I prepare myself to be just food for the worms

Skin

they thought he was a butterfly
he certainly acted like one
all of them like flowers lined up for him
and he enjoyed the sweet nectar from each one

in the dwam of love they forgot themselves
his skin started flaking and his trueself showed
they were still trapped in the spell he put them in

no more colorful wings but just empty grey
he was a moth and he started eating their clothes
they couldn't fight, for he was once their butterfly

no more nectar to enjoy
no more clothes to feed on
the moth craved for their flesh
so it is their corpse he ate

The Last Gospel

- death said,
'oh no dear, don't be afraid
I will carry you on my wings
we can fly over the unbounded sea
now wipe your tears,
I will hide you from your sins
we can be together beyond the horizon'

Travelers

two souls on two boats
in the ocean of my woebegone nights
with every stroke you make in the rippling waves
you move farther and farther
sitting still in my boat I'm slowly fading among the mist

two souls on two boats
want to be one yet two bodies pulling apart
two hearts moving away into the dark
becoming one with the waves and the mist of my woebegone nights

farewell traveler for we may never see each other again
you into the mist and I one with the belly of my ocean
as I slowly let go I will look for your hands waving at me
your trembling lips saying the last goodbyes

I wish you will see the land you seek
for I may only know the neverending cold of the ocean
I pray your trembling lips will wear a smile again
for I may only carry my misery on my pale face

farewell traveler for we may never see each other again

About Author

Jessin Jayan, born in 1998 in Kerala, India is a Bachelor's graduate in Hotel Management who currently resides in Wyoming, USA. He works as an Operations Manager full time but writing has been his passion from a young age. He has gotten many awards for his writing throughout his academic life. He established his first online presence in writing, by posting poems on Poetizer followed by publishing articles on Vocal.

Jessin's first published book 'Thoughts for a Woebegone Night' a collection of poems has released in 2024 as he works on his next book. You can find him hiking and fishing with his family when he is not writing. You can connect with him through his,

Instagram : @jayanjessin

Website : www.jessinjayan.com

www.ingramcontent.com/pod-product-compliance
Lightning Source LLC
Chambersburg PA
CBHW020244010526
44107CB00002B/94